SAMPO:
Heading Further North

For further information
on Bob Beagrie and Andy Willoughby,
please visit:
www.ekzuban.org.uk

Sampo:
HEADING FURTHER NORTH

Poems inspired by
Kalevala

BOB BEAGRIE

&

ANDY WILLOUGHBY

RED SQUIRREL PRESS

First published in the UK in 2015 by Red Squirrel Press
www.redsquirrelpress.co.uk

Red Squirrel Press is distributed by Central Books Ltd.
and represented by Inpress books Ltd.
www.inpressbooks.co.uk

Designed and typeset by Gerry Cambridge
gerry.cambridge@btinternet.com

A CIP catalogue record for this publication is available from the
British Library.

ISBN: 978 1 910437 04 9

Printed in the UK by Martins the Printers Ltd, Seaview Works,
Spittal, Berwick-upon-Tweed, TD15 1RS, on acid-free paper
sourced from mills with FSC chain of custody certification.
www.martins-the-printers.com

In loving memory of

PATRICIA MARGARET WILLOUGHBY

&

ELAINE TEASDALE

Foreword

IT MAY SEEM CURIOUS for two contemporary Teesside poets to engage with the national Finnish myth-cycle *Kalevala*. However, having taken part in a ten year performance, translation and publication exchange project with Finnish poets, including countless crazy adventures on the road, we have found that, as we gradually uncovered the various archetypes of Finnish mythology, it has struck a deep resonant chord within us in numerous ways, as has contemporary Finnish poetry and its fascinating poets.

Responding mostly to the first ten Runes of *Kalevala* we have attempted to examine the question of what it means to be an artist, how to confront and come to terms with loss of love and life, how our Northern and national identity connects to aspects of these myths, how our reading of the myths reinforced or challenged our sense of masculinity, how the present challenges the received ideas of the past, the relationship between humanity and mineral resources such as iron in ancient shamanic and modern secular cultures, and the price we pay for their use. The Myth of The Sampo, the undefinable object of healing properties, allowed us to explore the idea of a quest to find a healing magic in verse that informs our splintered British myths.

Throughout the sequence we have varied between contemporary re-tellings of key incidents within *Kalevala* and reflections at a contemporary tangent on the themes and archetypes thrown up by the myth, often relating them to personal memory or employing the use of 'poetic masks'.

By engaging with *Kalevala* we have been able to pursue the Sampo ourselves, both competing and working together, and like all grail quests we know this is bound to end in ultimate failure. However the quest justifies itself, we hope.

—*Bob Beagrie & Andy Willoughby*

Contents

Walking in Circles

The iron in the blood points North
The iron in the rocks stains 'em red
The blood in the hills drew iron
The iron from the hills cries blood
The North in the blood seeks iron
The North knows the origins of iron

Glad to escape the glare
of closed circuit cameras,
we climb through woods
toward the iron age fort
through oaks with rusted leaves;
concrete megaliths lost in ferns.
Sharp points of fresh, flowerless
scentless gorse, sentinel swords
each side of a ventilation shaft.
Beer cans and crisp wrappers,
a broken spade, mud stained rags.

The iron in the hills points North
The heather hides the village of Pit Top
A winch pin and a tin can lamp
The reed pools on the hills are blood red
The iron cools and sets in the pigs
The North knows the origins of iron

A fella used to live in there,
coming and going
like an apple of the forest,
dissenting hair, crazy beard
cottered with drays,
used to call him Nippa.
Harvester of mushrooms

berries and roots, eggs from the nest,
rabbits from a snare, the nuns
used to feed him jam and bread, others
claimed he lived on a diet of prayer;
from a bed of fern he'd watch
the flicker of the burn-off flares
over the encroaching town.

The iron in the hills points North
The hills in the North cradle iron
The slow river flows like molten iron
The iron flowed as thick as blood
The clouds rained black soot
The North knows the origins of iron

Twenty paces in the shaft is walled up.
It holds inside the hollow hill
the sour breath of the united dead,
but some little twats have knocked
a ragged hole in the brickwork,
to let in a shaft of curdled light
or release unconsecrated souls
to roam the dew heavy Yorkshire Mist,
the sodden Jurassic bracken
sprouting from black swathes
of twocca-set summer fires.

The iron in the blood points North
The iron in the hills drew blood
The blood in the iron sings North
The North in the iron points to blood
The pigs cool in domed steel shades
The North knows the origins of iron

In there lies Zulu, Kabul, Khartoum,
all those worldly lands of ransacked
Blue Billy, strata's of time,
precious remains and hollow men
sitting eating bait
in the sweating pitch
of fossilized eyeless fish.
Those emptied men with hardened shells
we stuff with the straw of history
to fill a lack of experience
we cannot buy gift wrapped for Christmas,
nor can we walk through the vaulted
chambers of their inverted Empire.

The iron in the blood points North
The shards of shattered hearts point North
The beard of the Viking chief points North
The prows of Whitby Whalers point North
The Reckoning begins in the North
The North knows the origins of iron

From the hill fort's circle above the town
with the worked-out whale belly below
unpick the dream of a muddy fish in the Baltic
with healing magic in her tones.

Head further North to suture
the wound from a steel edged lie,
where tongues freeze to railings in Winter,
where you will find a band of ragged poets
and circle the perimeter of this fort's twin
at Voipaala, hear rumours of a weeping wizard
who sought the secret origins of iron.
You make a vow with your blood brothers
to walk the quivering compass needle,
find the ferric song once beaten on the Sampo,
to salve this fractured land; these ransacked hills.

Northern Lullaby

Damp winter cold
groans in the bones,
asthmatic tubes
squeeze night tunes.

Try to surrender
to ursine hibernation urges.
Just lie still, let it pass, burn fat;

let the months disappear
into the dark cave
behind the eyes,

dream of Siberian reindeer
running in decreasing circles,
hooves striking through
snow onto hard permafrost

calling you to clean Northern air
that could take the last
whistling breath from your lips.

Bath Time

The gurgle of the plumbing brings
vague wonderings behind closed lids.
The sea's muffled voice in a shell
on the bathroom window sill
still singing its borrowed song;
not the bleating throat tones
of a benevolent lamb, dressed
and blessed for the high altar
but the deeper, restless rumble
of the Big Paw, Snuffle Snout,
a beady black eye in the spider plant.

Born to Float

I was born for this mystery:
The light-headed suspension
Between nothing and something
That is really nothing permanent.
I only knew my mother from the inside
And the sound that kept me in there
For what could have been a minute,
Nine months, a million years,
Was the lapping of wave on rock,
Of amniotic sea against womb lining
In counterpoint to an eternal heart
Whose deep beats still come to me
In half sleep, in the moment of song
That wells up from my drifting silence
When I feel myself on verge of disconnection
From the ephemeral solid forms around me,
The mamma beat, that tumbles and tosses
My words into meetings with origins
Of things, that allows me to create
And recreate them whatever it costs,
And all sounds, all things are born
Of this longing for the mother
Whose face remains unknown
To the conscious self,
Stopped floating.

Flotsam & Jetsam # i

from the bridge i watched the Northern Diver
from our letters duck down to disappear
spinning into the turbid Thames
taking her slippery memory in its beak

*

once cut loose from their moorings
        some myths malfunction
                rope burns
                        entangles
                                hangs us

*

the land is a scent caught
        within the curvature of each wave

*

the moth beating on her ceiling
comes back as i float
on my back with narrowed eyes
a ragged fluttering blots out the sun

*

lost to me
mammy shadowface,
out   of   focus
a rhythmic echo only

The Birth of The Shaman

It's a fact
we all come from the water
and
mothers imprison their children
to protect them from their future.

But what if
your mother was the ocean?
The ether's daughter—
surging vastness
of white-wreathed waves
and rolling billows
of storm-wind forces
flowing all directions
without a fixed abode.

She would,
(very likely)
hole you up safe
in the dark creases of her dresses,
in the softness of her bedding.
Swaddled in green tresses,
safe from scary monsters
one called Time
another called Ageing,
secured from joy and from sorrow;
kept blind as an oyster
locked within its shell.

To ease your restless longing,
to sooth tantrum tsunamis
she would sing the song of sunlight,
sing the silver moonbeams,
the islands full of shadows,

Father Ukko of the Thunder Home,
Honey Paw who prowls the sky.

You would dream and sleep
sleep and dream
and long to see these things for real
and beg and plead and cry and wait
for thirty years
for thirty years
you'd secrete a wish
as hard as pearl
as round as the promise
of a brave new world.

Would you give her the slip?
Would you
snap her heart in two?
As her first born son it is your job.
Would you
break the membrane
of your prison, creep out one night
when she wasn't looking?
Swim away like a worm
with no fixed abode?

Seven years I spent
in the drink,
the seedy underworld,
inventing a self
from submerged archives
of sponges, sea snails
creatures with pincers
and all those scaly fish.

I thought I was a fish myself,
a fish afloat, alive or dead.
I smelled like a fish—
a very ancient smell,
a strange kind of fish!
Man-fish, monster,
looking for the moon.
Singer
of the songs she'd taught me
in the cell of her womb.

Until the headland came in sight:
the promontory behind the surf,
the shifting dunes
with nesting birds
between the knees of boulders,
long-billed waders
wandering reed beds,
white towels draped over
the backs of empty loungers.

I swam into shallow waters
found my feet
walked onto land
and felt the beach ball sun
stroke my water-wrinkled skin.

Do the Float

In the city you can do it
with traffic all around you
with whore's and beggar's voices
inviting you to business,
after three days drinking
in dark and sea green caverns,
after hours of wandering
when all forms lose distinction
and strange faces are familiar,
when your dreaming is unleashed
from its daytime moorings
and streets noises are all merging
to a rhythmic babble,
underpinned by drumming
that resounds through
space, constantly vibrating.

Do the float, love,
let nothing touch you
or bring you to the pain
and sense of self.

Not the call of seagulls
on the rainy South Bank,
or the sudden light's glint
on St Paul's Cathedral,
or the great white palace
or the smell of frying onions
from the stalls of backstreet vendors
or the comic quacking of a Thames
mallard in ruffled alarum,
or the sharp words in the tavern
that bring grief and disillusion,

or the random burst of violence
that shocks you back to knowing,
or the sudden noticed neck nape
on the escalator, that's
heartbreakingly familiar.

Do the float, love,
through lost streets
with historic names
that now lead nowhere.

With wonky signs of shops
that really sell you nothing.
with tiny children chanting
obscenities or nonsense
in the city with its shifting name
Of London, Helsinki
Moscow, Kyoto
Amsterdam and Carthage.

Past old lepers and young lovers,
past invisible wheels of commerce,
past mind into non-mind
where loss becomes subsumed
into dreamtime longing -
where seasons are all one
and the dead begin their singing
from the buried layers
of city under city
bone and dust Arias
with harmony from the unborn
and the beat breaks through familiar
and you are once again
floating, painless, thoughtless,
in the timeless sea of mother.

Flotsam & Jetsam # ii

feathers on the flood tide float by me
cormorant pelican and eider ducks
each one with love's lost fantasies
glued in the ruffled silk

*

when days are bound by threads of fog
noon is but the yolk of a crushed duck egg

*

at four in the morning
a king-size bed floats by
that you stopped from spinning
off the face of the earth
with your little foot against mine

*

the existential weight of a bare lump of rock
an empty crisp packet's wind-fueled dance
without the story there is only now
coming and going in timeless waves

The Shaman Spots his Rival

Squatting in the wreckage of my sledge
I see this fresh-faced joy rider's smile
and know our crash was no mishap.
Know, too, how he has come to test
himself against the old man of Wainola.

Here he struts in all his pomp, prancing
onto hard packed snow, preening
like some royal peacock, bragging
of his exploits, claiming he can charm
a nightingale down from its nest.

And if I am that old man of Wainola,
he has traveled all this way to meet me,
driven for days from the Northland
to see if the rumours are true, to see
if his songs can beat my runes.

So he starts to sing his spells
So he starts to chant his poems
So he starts to pluck his rhymes
So he starts to pound out rhythms
So he starts to show his powers

This young man has some natural talent
he can turn a phrase and cast an image
he can hold a note, recount a tall tale
he can draw on legends and rework a cliché
he has read broadly, he has some knowledge
and devoted many a long hour to his practice.

But his runes are based on information
his songs are wrought for entertainment

his shining stanzas don't pierce the surface
his lines lack the luster of understanding
his whole craft is built on misassumption

His verses are shards of a broken mirror
what he calls magic is sleight of hand.
So I stand and wait for his voice to falter
to take my turn to call upon the origins,
strip him bare and land him in the mire.

Up to the Neck in It

I give in, tap out.
The swamp is hungry for my bones
and this old man can wrestle with runes
like a sifu of Shaolin kung fu with forms
and I would like to swallow my words;
that always lead me into the thick of it,
though they've never let me down
quite like this before.

Change that tune.

There was once a singer (*me*)
who proudly sang all the truths
of the land and of the life
he had learned:

Every lock needs a key
Wherever there's smoke there's fire
And land fires generally
Move faster uphill than down
The world is not flat but round
And spins around the fiery sun
At approximately 108,000 km per hour

Here on the meadows of Wainola
we go head to head, no holds barred.
His piece of shit sledge is a right-off
after the crash and I play every trick in my book.

The light and the dark both rise in the East
A fox's home in the ground is a set
An eerie is the name of an eagle's nest
The most common rock on Earth is basalt

There is a Yew in Scotland over 5000 years old
There are more pigs than humans in Denmark
There are less than 7400 tigers left in the world
A human being uses two hundred muscles to walk

But there's something in his watery eye
that I just can't read. He calls my runes
nursery rhymes, old wives tales,
mere fragments of broken mirror.

There are only twelve letters in the Hawaiian alphabet
A gathering of crows is known as a murder
A viking would use an enemy's skull as a goblet
The collective noun for cats is a clowder
Two mature trees provide enough oxygen for a family of four
The wheelbarrow was invented by the Chinese
A frog can leap but a toad cannot, though
There is a type of toad that bears live young

Maybe I should have listened to our Mam
when she tugged me back, begging
me not to come, despite me winning
District Karaoke King two years running
and reigning captain of our pub quiz team.

A cricket's ears are on its front legs, just below the knee
London's population is estimated at 7.2 million people
It is forbidden to pluck the fruit of the poisonous tree
Tarnkappes are hats that turn the wearer invisible
77% of people who look at internet porn are male
A bag of crack is cheaper than a pack of cigarettes
The largest living creature on Earth is the Blue Whale
With a heart the size of a Volkswagen Beetle

I reel out a litany of facts, figures and lore
but this old bloke with a silver beard
and a broken sledge remains unperturbed
by the length and breadth of my knowledge
and simply waits for my voice to falter.

Francis Drake completed the circumnavigation
Of the Earth in the Golden Hind in 1580
The Devil snares souls on the hook of temptation
It's impossible to sneeze with your eyes open
The Big Foot's native name is The Sasquatch
The mud skipper is a fish that can walk on land
Chickens should never
        be counted
            before they
                hatch

Battle Rune

Let us begin with something small;
a seed, a fresh start, that's already a result—
more of a point upon a spinning wheel;
a seed is a perfect way of saying sorry
of starting the whole cycle again, and you,
Joukahainen, what seed do you see in yourself?

Look deeper. What is required to grow yourself,
to germinate, root and to sprout the first small
leaves and flowers of true knowing; the bling you
sport, is it rich soil from which to grow a result?
A spiraled shell lying dormant awaiting sorry
rainfall to trigger germination, turn the wheel.

Time is a shopping trolley with a dodgy wheel
steering you down the wrong aisle of yourself.
Before you know it you're at the check-out, sorry
you can't return to the fruit & veg for one small,
ripe avocado pear, that melt-in-your-mouth result,
missed, forever longed for, slipping away from you.

The trappings of silk and fur draped around you
are an external bone, protection from the turning wheel
of chance; make a guess and hope for a good result
or strip them off, reveal your own mystery to yourself.
From here the winter moon in the sky's ocean is small
enough to gift wrap and send with a note saying 'Sorry'.

What a challenge for such a proud man to feel sorry,
as you have yet to take stock of all the wrongs you
have done, the sacrifices of others, some big, some small?
Will Pride quench the Earth's deep thirst, oil the wheel?
Is this in your thoughts when you consider yourself?
You think you are what you know. What a hollow result!

Your songs will fall short of the desired result.
There lies my write-off and you have not said sorry.
Your charms will scratch only the surface of yourself
until pride notes those gaping holes in the world within you;
how knowledge is naught but the spokes of the wheel,
all you will ever do is inconsequential and small.

Now, having come to the plains of Wainola yourself
to outwit an old man who craves some small-sorry
peace, the seed result you harvest is but a buckled wheel.

Citizens of the Floating World

Leg it across this bridge lads! It's the closest
we can get to running through the forest
or floating next to lilies in lake water—
all the people with umbrellas and faces
that have somewhere to get to in a hurry.
Not the faces of the dead but the right-now living
as we wander idle as night dwellers, minstrels,
who, in the city of Edo kept company with geishas,
clowns, and in Paris—Lautrec's tarts and dancers
in the red light of La Moulin, because the bard
doesn't sing now round the campfire but plays
for his whiskey pennies in the dark's refuge.
Look! Our faces so different to these parapluit people,
because in this rainy daytime we are refugees:
displaced Citizens of the Floating World.

The Poet's New View

He feels the slow, greedy suck of the swamp,
boots like sinking boulders
seeking something solid to stop the slide.

Any attempt to wriggle or reach for firmer ground
lands him inches deeper in the shit,
the cold press of earthy-water on his chest.

Beard bedraggled, mouth clogged with pond weed,
teeth entangled with lily pads,
he makes bargains with the rising skyline.

He thinks of a stumbling mastodon
that long ago met a similar death
drowned in the ring of its own supplications.

He sees himself, a small boy on thick lake ice
peering through a jagged fishing hole
dropping in a pebble he'd carried from the shore.

What other things might that ice hole require,
as well as the slug on its hook,
one horse shoe, an arrow head, his sister's doll?

Flotsam & Jetsam # iii

murky questions slide
      jump for pond skaters and flies
           leaves spreading rings,
                the widening eyes of memories

*

i opt to sleep in your cellar my friends
cave for the wintering bear or deep sea cavern
where tides erase memory and the drowned speech
of lovers fossilises into emerald coloured rocks

*

the lie of denial slipped out
as easy as spitting cherry pips
though we both knew it for what it was
she shook her head *You're all the same*
i never saw her again

*

clad in the blue-black armour of a colony
of mussels the rotting keel of the wrecked skiff
has proved itself too eager to steer towards strife

Vaino's Reflection

And I am older than the ancient oak
I once sowed in the soil as an acorn
way back in my prime and saw it felled
by a dwarf who rose from surf to become
a giant, and sweet Aino was a wild stream
or a shooting sapling beside a fresh spring's
trickle running headlong from the dawn;
already one of the rivulets of tears
that poured from her mother's eyes.
All she could see in me was age,
the hard ridged bark of so many years,
the sag of the skin, my long grey beard,
how these chapped, calloused hands
would rasp like sand on her silken cheek.

Brother

He said I had no faith,
where, he asked, *was the family support?*
If only I'd persuaded him to stay.
The day he left we fought, tooth and nail,
like we hadn't done since that day
he denied stealing my favourite doll.
I slapped his face though he didn't flinch,
yelling, *pride comes before a fall.*
But Jouki would never let a thought lie
once it had planted roots in his mind.

And he could never bear the idea
that anyone could better him
at ice swimming, at sailing,
at drinking, at hunting, at singing.
He would much rather be boiled alive
than not be the last to leave sauna.
And when he heard the rumours
of this minstrel of Wainola,
who could sing a change in weather
wake the bears from winter slumber
make trees bow down their boughs
weave dreams with threads from rainbows,
poor Jouki couldn't sleep.
He'd wander, brooding, through the house,
for days I hardly saw him eat.

He set off due South on his sleigh
to return in a week in a terrible state
blabbering on about quicksand
the death of a woolly tusker
and apology after apology,
till the truth of it all came out

like heaving vomit, once started,
hard to stop, though I wanted
nothing but to stuff his mouth
with wool, to cover up my ears.

He has married me off
as a kitchen slave, to save his skin,
to an old cold fish whose idea of love
is carefully tending to all his needs,
picking up his sweaty socks
braiding my hair just for him
binding tight my wild heart
waiting on him hand and foot
soothing his brittle temper
being seen, but not being heard
especially when he's thinking
especially when he's wrestling
with the lines of his poems, and
spreading my legs at his command.

Unthinking the Ocean

Damn you! Be quiet, can't you see I'm unthinking the ocean?
Why do you distract me with your biscuits and your kisses?
I was nearly in the zone beyond sense in the lapping of the
    waters.
Don't bug me with your talk about a holiday or romance—
this is a serious business, this mantra to merge into origins.
How am I supposed to turn back the waves or walk on fucking
    water?
Yes I know my bastard feet are wet but I'm not going to catch
    my death.
Damn it! There's no need for that kind of cruel language—
nobody said anything about anyone leaving for anywhere.
What are you bringing that old shit up for—you always have to
    ruin it!

The Wizard's Wooing

First he sent her a candle flame
that flickered without a wick
along with three simple scrawled
instructions on how to keep it lit.
Next he sent her the splintered tip
of a forked lightning bolt, lodged
fizzing in a nugget of pure blue calcite.
Then he sent a still living bee
that had long ago lost its sting.
The next day its tiny barbed scimitar
came in a box with a solid smoke ring,
inscribed around its inner rim—
the secret ingredients for chlorophyll.

With each new gift's arrival
Mother fussed and crooned.
Dad showed them off to the neighbours,
but the familiar view of fens and fallows
gentle meadows around the lake, where
she'd pick ferns and flowers, chase
butterflies in Summertime and follow lines
of ants to their hills, all tumbled into the sea;
what remained were bogs and stubble, stunted trees
boulders blasted by Arctic winds, by acid rain,
and a lost girl with hands running red,
her voice the caw of a hungry crow.

She watched Arto standing on a floating islet
waving, yelling and vanishing down
the wrong end of a telescope, along
with the promises they had made
when they'd carved each other's names
into the silver skin of an old birch's trunk

with the sharpest blade on his penknife.
When he'd shrunk to the size of a crumb,
a wriggling maggot waiting for a hook,
she stretched, and realised it was her who
had been catapulted far out of reach,
her that had shrunk to the size of a larvae
and the pain in her chest was the hook
meant to snag the lip of Wainola's old fish.

Flotsam & Jetsam # iv

a doll made from a frayed sock
floats a jellyfish bob in icy currents
does it remember the toes the heel?

*

the park stripped by January's bleak faces
i stood beside a thicket of dried wrinkled berries
in coat gloves and scarf crunching ice under boot
watched her help her little sister scramble
onto an elm tree's low branch and knew
with a calmness of that winter's spaces
i'd stepped into a puddle called love

*

midsummer Sun
burns the skin
around my eyes
as i forget
the way your skin
felt at my fingertips

*

the discarded beam of an ornate plough
once cut deep furrows through richest meadows
and forever lined its owners brow

Called into Knowing by the Land of Your Body

I floated on and on wordless in the language of sound.
At night the waves slurp-slapped against red granite
And the wind whistled soft through invisible reeds.

The waters round me were thinning intangibly.
I heard the sound of spring birds, geese arriving,
All sounded through me but still I did not stir,

I floated on and on languid in the passing of years,
Dreaming in sound and cloud as my time disappeared
And the final drift into the dark grew ever closer.

Then a chance wave brought me up against your heat,
The warmth of your foot against my cold hard knee
I awoke in the glow of your fertile pale skinned island.

You called up songs from my floating babble,
Allowed me to weave the weft of the word-hoard,
I planted green trees and watered them to blossom.

On the slopes of your mountains I sang freely—
I was an eagle in the plunge of your valleys
In a swoop of pure being that seemed endless.

I whispered you into the cradle of summer sleep
But I had failed to sing you free of father sadness
The right words lost in the floods of mother longing.

And when I wandered away to seek knowledge
I left your heat and your storm force too easy.
The earth shifted in its hard diurnal courses—

You shifted from hot flesh to cold fish skin,
Swam deep to the bottom of the chill sea
Serenaded forever by the voices of the drowned.

In the Land of Lumiukko

First hints of Spring, while packed snow thaws,
the fixed grimace of each lake begins to thin
and forest palvi appear, I wrap up in fur
to slip past the sleeping faces of my kin
unlatch the door and leave the familiar lair
for good. Out in gloom, before the weak dawn
I listen to the wind, the slump of snow's fall
from sagging branches in the blackness,
and the tin sky aglitter with indifferent stars,
ground frost shining its crisp, silver flatness.
I pass the rugged snowman by the driveway
pick up his hat, push it back onto his head.
His prehistoric eyes will not dance today
his smile, along with his scarf, has fled
across the field's soft sweep to the road.
This man, like the rest, is dead in the chest,
nothing beats there but a cold-blooded toad.
This 'Love'—their word, doesn't stand the test
against desire, against stature or survival.
So I make for the road, turn from the village.
My boots crunch a rhythm of disapproval.
Laululintu, fleeing the ornate safety of its cage
to find its wings clipped, plucked, frostbitten.
I cry icicles for a world ruled by snowmen.

What the Hare Heard

I am big eye of the rolling meadows
Having run through shrinking shadows.
I am swift foot among the flowers
Having raced the diving swallows.

I am long leg of the cornfields
Having darted, chased by rennies.
I am moon dancer in the graveyard
Having borne a tale upon my ear tips.

For I caught her clear as a cut glass bell
Weeping through the sandy dunes,
Saw her with my big bright eye
Walk straight into the deep wet swell.

For I listened with a long straight ear
To her splashing out toward the waves
And talking to the water maids
Who washed her tears with salty sea.

For I saw her reach a rainbow rock
And scramble upon its gnarly top,
I heard a crash and watched it drown
Saw waters slap above her crown.

That's how Aino became the surf spray
I cannot swim, so I could not help!
Aino's bones have turned to sea shells
Her golden hair is deep, green kelp.

Her voice now echoes in salmon caves
Muffled beneath the glittering waves
Like a lost and lonely cuckoo's pleas
Within a shimmering sea of silver leaves.

No Such Thing as Bad Weather
Arto's song

They called off the search after five days with no lead
and when the missing posters began to fade
arranged a memorial service for anyone who cared.

I watched the proceedings from behind the wheel,
at a distance crows stalked daisy damp mounds
the priest's words a spade's dull thud in turf.

People shivered, stamped and complained
about the weather. How they shook their heads.
The TV reporters and their camera crew left.

At her wake in Pohjola Cafe I climbed inside
a bottle and sipped grief into senselessness.
It made no sense that she left no note.

It wasn't like her to go without saying goodbye.
She was bound to show up at any time
in her usual late fluster, pour me a coffee,

scribble an order for a cheeseburger
and laugh her door-bell-tinkle-giggle about
the most recent antics of Luna, her Arctic fox.

I caught your eye before you cast it back
rolled it along the road from the village.
These days you can't look anyone in the face

with your blue-eyed-boy's cracked mask.
What happens now? Where do we go from here?
I trace names carved into the bark of our tree.

I spot her eyes in knots, feel her cold lips in moss
catch her smell in deserted corners,
her voice calls out from running water.

Rumour has it it's all down to your mouth
in the first place, and to think you once
warned me off as a complete waste of space—

You're not fit to lick the boots of a girl like Aino!
but would I have offered her up as ransom?
Sometimes rain falls sideways, snowflakes rise.

The Floating Man

I cannot say *forgive me* or explain my distance
when you are already gone back to the waves:
where faces meet with faces in the endless flow

on the up and down escalators and in reflections,
in the big shop windows and empty pint glasses
on the tables of the dimly lit taverns I'm adrift in.

I cannot say *I was driven by my longing*
or the inner urge of understanding to feel
my way around the fragments in the ooze

of the cracked egg that all was born from.
Driven to catch hold of a broken slice of moon
or the sun on an ice cube in the boat bar,

when I should have kept my eyes on you—
all sun and moon held in your open palms
offered me as I floated and scribbled oblivious.

I can't say, *sometimes I am this other floating man,*
who waited thirty years to be cast into being,
enchanted by a rhythm in the push and pulling waters

of the city's hidden rivers, far below the streets,
that makes me seem an aged son of winter
even in the pink flush of your dancing summer.

Who, on the perfect island alone with you
by silver birch and pine surrounded,
sat atop a rock to stare for hours at the ocean

in untouchable far away melancholy.
I can't say *this is not past loss I'm holding onto,*
but the Floating Man come back to being,

who cannot treasure the instance of yourself,
as all is merged and rocked into the eternal.
By the time the clock comes back our time is over.

It does no good to say *I noted all your secret places;*
that now the birdlike movement of your little hands
holds sway amongst the flow of beating fragments.

The One that Got Away

There comes a moment in any fool's life
when self pity burns like a fresh brand
blistering in the aftermath of mishap;
the whole sky comes tumbling down
in a disbelieving torrent. That's me
with a fish knife standing in the skiff
knowing I'd lost her not once but twice.
The fair fish gone with a flick of the tail
and daylight cracked by a gull's outcry,
each swell a shard of glass reflecting
the face of my fiancée from Pohjola.
I wanted nothing from that moment
but to return to the hopeless floating
I'd once struggled so hard to escape.

Be Careful What You Fish For

You may catch the unexpected and miss the only moment
to bring back the holy second or the sacred being of love.
If you have numbed your heart and obscured your secret eye
the truth may wriggle from your fingers and flip into the depths
until the form becomes nothing in the murky waters,
spirals away with a part of you that may not be retrieved;
leaving you just words to bring back the moment's phantom
never again living within the compass of your fingers;
not able to be brushed with your buzzing lips' antennae.
And this is how I held her but did not see to know her,
saw all her pretty parts but failed to recognise my lover
as I tried to place her in the lists of those gone before.
When it meant slicing her wide open for cold-eyed study,
she flipped away and swam to hotter hands across the ocean.

Shaman Song

I can sing light with the knowledge of bird heart and feather
So wings sprout for a moment from the backs of my listeners

I can sing the cold vast mass of primeval stones
Until the world around me takes on the state of crumbling slate

I can sing the wind in the Baltic reeds around the islands
Into a symphony to soothe the heart of the raging bear king

I can sing the sea into a winter thickening despite its salt
So I can walk across the archipelago in my snowshoes

I can sing the solid earth into soft sucking quicksand
Beneath the feet of bumptious rivals for the bard's crown

I can sing a village into a town and a town into a city
And with a chosen word or trumpet sound bring them all down

I can sing a single spark into a raging forest fire
Reduce all behind me into black wasteland for the enemy

I can conjure tears as broad as beans from young lover's eyes
Remake the last sound of a cruelly wounded hart

I swear on a good day I can turn a hill into a mountain
And cover its steep slopes with lush green forest

All these things were given me in the floating dreamtime
But sing as I will, I cannot bring you back from the deeps.

Flotsam & Jetsam # v

storm rinsed relics
        lost Moomins
torn tasselled dresses
and King Eriuc's screams of madness

*

she dared me to walk away from her in thick fog
if it's meant to be we'll find each other she said
and she was right but when we did it was over
she knew i hadn't believed it
        —too entranced by the lapping
of the invisible ocean in the dark's deep harbour

*

we first noticed the properties of iron
        embedded in a wolf's paw print
right there the promise of a keener sting

*

flat sodden figures almost indistinct
paint almost erased by baltic salt
chagall's blue kiss in late August—
two lovers free from the grip
of the work-weary world
promised a glimpse of pure heaven
should've known you old fool
one of them was hiding a blade

*

between precarious ledges
the greening skull of an impatient heifer
that wasted its milk in running away

Vengeance

Watching slow mist slide over the water,
swimming from tree to tree this jealous morn.
Beading the moss of the rocks on the shore,
weighting spider webs strung from road signs.

I sit at the open window
listening to the jarvi's lap,
the knock-knock of the boats.

Who's there?

Between the watching and the listening
I work at the crossbow: sanding ash,
stretching sinew, inlaying silver, weaving flax,
paint a bounding hare and a sleeping girl.

Seven bolts I feather with loving care,
dip each point into a pot of adder's spit
for the patient day the enchanter comes,
riding a courser across fog heavy water.

Sweet Just Desserts

I told you, some day, he was sure to come.
Didn't I say it was just a matter of time
Before his longing got the better of him,
Once his loneliness outweighed his grief

He'd head Northward sniffing out a wife.
Did I tell you how I had been waiting:
Through all those days of watching
Through all those nights of listening

Through hours of her lost voice singing,
Under the eye of the stuffed, mounted hare
The days of quiet working in the boathouse
At Fog Point to make sure he meets his maker?

Oh but, Mam, you should have been there!
You should have seen my steady aim
Once I'd sighted his charger's canter
Through the lake shore's sunlit mist.

The first time my bowstring buzzed
The feathered ash-bolt raced too high
And vanished into steamy billows.
I made adjustments and drew again.

My second shot was aimed too low
The bolt struck firm into the sandy bank
From where Aino and I learned to swim
(by the jetty where she would push me in).

But the third one, Mam, was on its mark
I heard the thud, saw his charger stumble.
The bolt struck near his golden girdle.
He plunged face-first into icy ocean.

When I paddled over to the killing point
There were blood trails drifting on the surface.
Mother, I've whacked the old man of Wainola,
Sent him off to the grim kingdom of Tuonela.

Back in the Drink Again

'Thus he wept for two and three nights
For as many days stood weeping,
For the country round he knew not,
And no path could he discover,
Which perchance might lead him homeward
Back to a familiar country'
—Kalevela: *Runo IV*

Check this out—a hundred wounds from all that stuff in the
    float.
Bites and scratches from half familiar nails and prows of
    rowing boats.
Look at this in the half-haunted shafts of yellow street
    lamplight,
a water-stained picture from the days when all seemed right.
Who was she mate? Well, you might well ask but I'll not reply,
For fear I can't recall or this weeping will wrench me till I die,
Just buy me another one love—by the banks of the great brown
    river.
Ignore the ancient boatman's call don't say you saw me shiver,
What if I take your sage advice dear, in kindly foreign tones,
and find the magic rhythm to heal my wounds and take me
    home?
To find all changed forever while I have wallowed in the booze,
the houses boarded up, buddies all dead from the blues?
Which river is this? Which lake? Where are the ducks in the
    park?
I have lost track of the needle in the compass of the heart.

The Ever Float

Like salmon
we all return from whence we came:
a particle of moisture in a cloud
droplets on a water wheel
light rainfall on the mountain top.
I've drifted as a willow twig out into open sea.
That bolt from nowhere killed my steed,
launched me from the saddle
in a fall that shook all thought from me.
The bitter sea wipes clean all memory
refills my skull with rush and surge,
with glimmers of epiphany.

I drove a rag & bone cart piled high
with mistakes and some mistook my cargo
as wisdom: a broken bike, smashed TVs,
stepladders without the rungs, snapped
fishing rods, clapped-out rusted engines;
the things that most throw out as junk
I'd take away as basic truths.

This weightless amnesia takes my toe nails
webs my fingers, grows me fins and gills.
I gulp the sun, sip the sweat of starlight—
stars being stallions straining at their reins.
I lap up moonbeams and peel my eyes
for an eagle's flight among the clouds.
As a fallen leaf upon the tide I float
in all directions with no fixed abode.

Floating Away

'In an age where all is fleeting.
Shall I rear in wind a dwelling
Build a house upon the waters?
If I rear in wind a dwelling
Then the wind would not sustain it
If I build a house on water,
Then the waves will drift it from me'
—Kalevela: *Runo IV*

I have wept for the familiar on the edge of a strange country
Though in my homeland I have never settled in a dwelling.
The restless pull of moon and the surging need to know
Has pulled down the walls of each easy dwelling domicile
And left me starving once again floating on the oceans
With a hundred wounds licked at by tongues of salty water,
With my hair in disarray and my parched lips hardly singing
Carried beyond the comfort of familiar homely voices.

I have woken in strange cities as I tried to make the Sampo
That would give me the knowledge to bring love back home.
I have seen neon skyscrapers light up with sudden adverts
From a hard bench bed in a shirt soaked with blood.
I have stood upon twin towers and looked out to the island
Where Liberty's Lady offers the elusive torch of freedom.
I have journeyed North till my eyes swept across the taiga;
Endless plains waiting silent for the bite of bitter winter.

I have come to in little bedrooms to hear the songs of strangers
Full of fiery potions that sent me city drifting;
Felt limbs warm against mine in lost hours after midnight
Knowing there was no time left for them to gently hold me
Before I was swept out by the tide of the day's dawning
To seek the secrets for the sacred Sampo's final forging
In greasy breakfast joints with a view of ancient rivers,
Or in rainy morning parks with the plain trees softly weeping.

Yes, I know it's possible to lose me in the midst of conversation
When the floating comes upon me and time begins to circle
Like the eagle that may lift me from the tide of wordless babble
To drop me on new shores where I am once again a stranger.
Forgive me if you lost me before our story was concluded
I was born to the float where all plots are lost to the whirlpool
Before they can come to any kind of catharsis or conclusion,
Believe me, I did not wish to be this bringer of confusion.

When I find the Sampo I will sing you a sweet homestead.
I will see you but never try to break you down to list you,
I will stop weeping in my beard for years so swiftly passing,
I will stop the river flowing and turn back the angry oceans.
When I forge the sacred drum I will dance the heavens open
You will see me cloaked in lightning, soaked in starlight,
Your eyes will blaze when you tango in my magic's rhythm
My knee between your legs, my song so deep within you.

But for now, my love, the tall pine trees they still pierce me
The birches whip the flesh from my strained bent back,
My friend the wind still seeks to serenade me to the Sampo,
She blows across my mind like the feathers of the swan.
The sun dances light on frozen lakes to entice me
From the urge to go forever floating into darkness:
The Great Bear offers me his roar, his strength and sisu
To find the iron within me, pointing North to a reckoning.

The Unhealed Wound

I would have done anything to please you, anything you asked
my new love, with your small demands and your secret frailties,
your trail of broken hearts and your line of hidden suitors.
I split horse hairs with a blunt knife and the strop of my wit,
I tied eggs into knots for you, performed no end of tricks
I peeled stones like oranges, carved ice without breaking it
but when I tried to carve the boat to finally take you home
the axe went astray when my mind was in the float.
Ill spirits filled the gap between us, drove the blade into bone,
to make a wound that won't stop bleeding in fast-gushing flows.
I can find a song to make the icy waters turn to steam,
I can find a rhythm to make storm clouds dance and billow,
but I do not know the origin of the iron to undo its evil being.
So I withdraw, head North to check my rushing bloodstream.

Flotsam & Jetsam # vi

drifting in a rock pool
the shaft of a snapped cross bow
that grinned whenever it killed

*

will you go out with me?
i almost added, *please*
She looked so sad, her cluster
of school friends stood shocked
before starting to giggle
i already knew the answer
and walked away to hide

*

on a brand new beach
a faded map of a coastal village
that's already slipped beneath the rising sea

*

the box of chocolates
burned my fingers
where it touched the skin

*

first ice in the water
thickens the fluid around me
immobile in the float
the frost whitens my beard

The Quest

Billy Billy Billy
Come on out Billy Boy!

And tell me the secrets of the town
that cast me in its image,
made me ripe for this wound.

Yell into the hole in the hollow hill.
If you listen to the babble behind the echo
you hear the voices of crushed miners
coaxing and cursing
the manganese iron ore.

Billy Billy Billy
Come on out Billy Boy!

And the chattering of lost tribes
with their tales of the iron's birthing
from the still water's bedding.
How it formed a dolorous spear
to slice a wound of endless flowing,
to split a stone and run for cover.

And somewhere beyond the fallen shafts
beyond the flooded chambers, named
for long gone glories of Imperial Battle,
a recalcitrant milky whisper
of the stone's last remnants
in Abandonment's dusty corners.

Billy Billy Billy
Come on out Billy Boy!

That I now remember hearing
on the ruined slopes of Rapala
as the Finn bard Kalle told us
how that iron age fortress
prevented Viking slaughter.
And now I'm Vainamoinen
consulting the wizened healer:
recalling Ilmarinen's seduction
of the most reluctant iron
to his smithy's starving fire,
to his impatient primal anvil.

Billy Billy Billy
Come on out Billy Boy!

The Smith & The Iron

Brother, I see you hiding in the wild wolf's print,
Spilt milk from the breast of the mother of rust.
I know your fear of the red fire chamber,
Know too the scare of losing form to flow,
But it's high time to tease you from the swamp.
My arts will only let you gain in beauty
My forge will help you find your full strength,
With heat and hammer I'll bring you into Being.

Leave me be, don't interfere, I'm fine where I lie
At the edge of the swamp covered by brackish water,
In the pack's prints and sunken dents of bear.
One day I could become anything, serve good or ill
But leave me here where the frost may chill
My restless form and make me hard and unknowing
As a common stone in your own home's hills.
Now fuck off back to that palookaville!

Have you seen yourself? Take a long hard look.
Your coarse, outer form requires some fashion,
Just to bring out your inner splendor,
Just to enhance your natural glamour.
Under my hands, Brother, you could shine like a star.
What is blunt can be sharp, what is tainted can be pure.
Let me wash away the grime of eons
My tools, my skills, shall place you in the spotlight.

Well it's true I've been out of the light too long
And my soul is finer than my thuggish looks allow,
But I know your sort with your interplanetary plans
You just want to trade my talent for quick cash in hand
You want to waste me away in the furnace fire,
Pass me onto murderers, fools and liars

With no chance to return to this lake land's quiet edge
Where songbirds can calm me from the waving sedge.

That's not my game, but it's a risk worth noting.
In the wrong hands and with a gnawing grudge
Your tapered edge could slice man's flesh
Far easier than cleaving stone and chopping wood.
That's why I first require from you a promise
Before I transform a frog into a prince,
You shall vow never to turn against your maker
Nor your maker's brother, father, mother, child.

Hypocrite man, you pretend your motives are fine.
When your kind try to dig me from the earth
There's a costly lesson you will never learn—
You can't dictate my purpose once I'm gone for sale
Then it's me you blame for the widow's bone chilled wail.
I have no desire to serve for good or ill,
But if you can bind me safely as you now foretell
For fame's sake I'll suffer the flame's hot spell.

The Hornet's Song

I, the black and yellow bird of Hiisi, set the smith to suffer.
So simple it was to slip a sac of poison into the smelt:
A single drop from a rattlesnake's striking fangs.
In the second they stabbed and opened twin wounds
Added a smattering of red ant's searing acid,
The snapping mandibles of relentless soldiers,
Some coronary inducing quinine
Sucked from bubbling toad skin.
And the *piece de resistance*, the monstrous moonshine—
The distilled seething avarice of ordinary men.
Now you blame the blade you so diligently fashioned
For slaking its thirst from the veins of your weeping friend,
And all those who seek to follow the magnetic iron
That hides in the heart and the lungs' dark cellars.

Ferrous
Song of the Transformed Iron

This morning, brimful with strength and shine
I am the ubiquitous re-enforcer of the heavy Rule of Law,

of security glass, foundations hidden under your feet.
Harnessed stone of sky-dust and cooled earth core.

Supporter of rooftops and the foliage of street signs over
your bowed, obedient heads; while you remain hoodman blind.

You promised me I would become the Shining One,
And true enough I have been the perfect gentleman,
As the sun glinted me I pricked out a dying wail
From punctured guts of men in the mud at Passchendale.

Flesh piercer of your sour dreams, reflecting sunlight,
around the roads you ride, turning the tire-wrapped grind

on the clockwork cogs of machines. Silent conductor of
     electricity,
conveyor of heat and cold, the cargo on tracks that hum and
     groan.

But I recall the weight and dark of the petrescent seam
in the roots of hills, where I lodged as rough blue stone.

As crude crafted blade I sliced through skin for sacrifice,
carved brave-hearts from enemies on your hill fort site.
As arrowhead I danced in perfect flight as dawn broke
at Voipaala and Odin's boys were caught up in my sights.

Remember how I bubbled like simmering soup in the smelter,
     aglow
like a sun in a saucepan and flowed in runnels to set—purified,

You thought. Now my bite slides into waiting locks to turn oiled
tumblers, smooth bed-head cotters, secure a cell door to a lie.

All around I abide, a bridled slave in shackles, to scrape chins,
smooth legs, stab peas, spoon, scoop, drill, lever, lay still and
   spin.

I evolved into razor wire to protect you from your brother,
I am the quick flicking tongue that steals the heart of mothers.
As winding curling barbs I keep camp inmates in,
I am the starving one fuelled forever by your sin.

For you I span river banks, touch cloud, turn soil in furrows
yet this thirst for life is a driving curse. No mere whim.

I never wanted this—it's plain, with my recalcitrant inertia.
You hammered out my shape but you can't control my dance.

On a sheet of recycled paper I form the letters for forgiveness
as a fine ink tipped nib. Venom burns. I simply drink for release.

A Charm to Still the Flow

'Everything flows and nothing abides;
Everything gives way and nothing stays fixed.'
—Heraclitus

Tell me the spell to stop the flowing.
With all things still. With all things still.

How to hold back the trickle, the drip of the glacier
that begins the flood, the rise of tides
that turn the float into a surfer's hell ride,
with flotsam & jetsam transformed
into a thousand hurtling fragments?

> Hold fast as a concrete breakwater
> Against the river's Springtime swell

> Or a glass figurine of a flamenco dancer
> La Duende humming through each contour

> Or a half sunken boulder in moorland peat
> Impervious to the lash of winter gales

Tell me the spell to stop the flowing.
With all things still. With all things still.

How to save me from the salted wound
and the incarnadine ocean with its whirlpool
that drags under the last shadow face
of an unknown mother, amongst splintered
timbers from Endeavour, Kontiki,
the weeping poet's skiff and Ahab's peg
from the whale rendered Pequod?

Stem it with an ice-locked lake in the middle
Of a night that will last thirty arctic days

Or the sea-halted flow of red magma
Quickly cooled to basalt grey

Or a carved mountain's face in a hurricane
Preserved in the dour leader's vinegar dignity

Tell me the spell to stop the flowing.
With all things still. With all things still.

How to dam the surging black cataract of Tuoni,
full of dismembered memories, a lock
of Lemminkäinen's hair, a wooden crucifix;
mementos from the Urals, Tampere and Cantabria,
a hyperactive rainstick, Kerouac's pulled daisy
and Dry Tom's geranium, a sharp wooden
pyramid from the state-sponsored chambers
of Thomas Torquemada?

Freeze its cruel revolution with an insomniac's
Eternal 3.30 in the morning

Or the fixed, distanced weight
Of a morbid week's anticipated news

Or with the judder of elasticated space
In the instant of a car crash

Tell me the spell to stop the flowing.
With all things still. With all things still.

How to pause the electronic tsunami
with its pirate sack of pop-ups selling chocolate

cocks, debt relief and lascivious chat lines;
sexy Suvi offers head while your eyes fixate
on the charred, black arm stumps
of a boy named Collateral.

> Block it with the cold and warm subjects' repose
> In a pin hole camera's lens
>
> Or a sturdy flagpole rooted in the lake bed
> To warn the unwary hauki hunter
>
> Or the last romantic pose of the left handed gun
> Head cocked to the right on a wanted poster

Tell me the spell to stop the flowing.
With all things still. With all things still.

To stifle the poisoned screams of the molten steel
and the half sunk trunk of a son fallen in
from the furnace's open lip, pushed down
and silenced by his father's rod
in the name of Mother Mary's mercy.

> Suspend yourself with the magnetic pull
> Of two equidistant poles
>
> Stretch out your arms like a scarecrow
> On the ley lines running East to West
>
> Let the Shaman pierce your chest and hoist
> You dangling in the holy Sun Dance

Tell me the spell to stop the flowing.
With all things still.
With all things still.
With all things still.

Guilt Trip

You look worn and wiped out, my friend.
Clock-off for a well earned break?
You've become wizened by the heat
of the flames you tend. This cool bottle
of vodka will slake your parched throat,
rest your sore bones, we have new
wild plans and preparations to make.

Pah! I have precious metals to draw
from the stone, as if I've got the time
for another wild goose chase. Give up
your quest Vaino, just head for home.
We're far too old to go off roaming
about the place. My roaring forge
is the world's fecund womb. I'm happy
right here, blessed by her fire's grace.

Ilmarinen, Ilmarinen, this place is more
like a tomb! Come on, let's head off
North to the cold, we should go hunt
a sacred bear and flirt with doom. Oh,
and there's a maid up there dripping
with gold, copper and silver that'd match
even your finest work, and the sparkle
in her eyes entices young and old.

It's your eyes on her assets you silver
bearded berk. I bet her arse is ample,
her dowry impressive. I'll not down
these tools to put on a fancy shirt.
You need my craft to woo her, you
moaning manic depressive as your songs
will make her weep or fall fast asleep,
whining for your Mammy's tit
like some chronic regressive.

Look closer at my wound, Smithy,
though it's ceased to weep with a charm
to stop the blood, first I learned the secret
of the venom in the blade that made
it bite so deep. It was all your mistake,
your lack of care, don't forget, that cast
the curse over your own craftmanship.
Now make amends, forge the Sampo.
Repay the debt.

The Trouble with Wizards

Is that they always over reach the grasp of their magic
and it's us smiths of the world who have to save their heads
when they promise a dream they can never deliver.

'Just make me a Sampo for Louhi,' he says,
The gap toothed witch of Pohjola
'So I may wed her daughter and we can all go home.'

'Make it from the tips of swan's white wing plumes'
Yeah, right Man, *'and from the milk of a barren heifer,
and from a single grain of barley,'* Well I ask you,
'and from the fleece of a summer sheep.'
As if any fool can do it.

'Make me something brand new,' he says, *'Something
never seen before and never to be seen again.'*

As if that's not enough the daft old bard
wants the witch *'to play the drums on it'*,
wants it *'to store grain from the South for the Winter,
grind corn from the West for barter, mint coins
from copper and silver'* to keep his wife in her customary bling.

And to top it all *'it has to shine'*,
enough to warm the heart of a Northern ice queen
who has just traded in her daughter to a bloke
who spends most of his days weeping
for the lost poems of the world atop a Baltic rock.

Nice One!

So muggins here says just show me to the anvil.

It's a piece of piss for the man who forged the heavens,
who carved the vault that holds the air
for all living things to breath in.

But there is no workshop, no hammers or tongs,
never mind a bleeding anvil, so I set myself to wander
in the mists of Sariola, till on a scrubby stretch of wasteland
I find a flat stone of many colours and build my forge beneath it.

Sampo Unbound

Is a form so hard, so cold, it can break the ice around the heart?
A form to save you, for a vital second, from the Ever Float.

Mix into the smelt a small vial of tears from lovers lost to the
    flow,
the stain of your bardic rival's spittle as he turns sour
in his quest to snatch your throne as King of The Empty
    Orchestra.

All the kingdoms of the Earth, condensed to powder—just add
    water,
all the crumpled wrapping paper from Christmas morning,
a rabbit's paw on a string, white goods and the cuddly toy.

Let it emerge from the forge's furnace as a greasy wrapper
of black makkara mixed from pearl barley and the blood
of a wounded wizard masquerading as lingonberry sauce,
to be devoured at dawn for comfort in a Salmiakki haze
after the walk of shame through Tampere market place
with Dr Gorilla and The Hang Over Fairy counting
the spare change they've lifted from your leaking pocket.

But what if it infects me with the mid-morning longing
for the shady bar and perfect glass of cool, cloudy Lonkero,
which could stretch into a lifetime lost in the Ever Float?

Smelt it down again and add the skull of a Karelian bear
that remembers Obugrian songs of apology
before the *karhunliha* was sliced into gutfuls of Sisu.

Chuck in the shanties of steel workers brought
from starving Eire, that echo in ghost halls of blast furnaces,
levelled and swept under the carpet at The End of History.

Draw it from the flames with scalded tongs as a golden disk
on a gramophone that plays the dust in its grooves
with the static of the Dead transfigured into song: let it sing
of the spirits that once lived in every tree and rock,
let it sing like Vainamoinen of the origins, let it sing
like William Blake that *everything that lives is holy.*

But what if it sings bitterly of bloody recompense
for lives laid waste to lay foundations of palaces
of Princelings and those implacable iron masters?

Smelt it down again and add half a magic stone
to keep your babies safe when you set out for Shangri la,
The City of Shambala and the Misty Isle of Avalon.

Offer up the talisman of a wedding band that's tapped
upon wood, stone and metal to divine a way back
out of the Northward Quest when the sea starts to set.

Let a Golden Woman step out from the flames
to sing a lay full of the End of All Longing,
woven from the single thread of spider's silk
that twitches the leaves to show wanderers a way
between the trees to the still, lily-kissed lake
for the morning swim through ripples of calm.

But what if she sings you a Siren Song, a song
to set you weeping through your beard for home,
so a sharp rock resembles your yearning pillow?

C'mon Smithy, toss in a Gideon's Bible pilfered from a motel
with a Playboy Bunny pasted in the Book of Revelation.
Throw in a dinosaur bone pissed on by weary poets,
in the Steppes of Siberia beside unfixed rail tracks.
The black walking stick topped with a dragon's head.

The claw footed picture of the Crow King of Rapala.
The howls of a hairy shaman beset by wood imps.
The burnt lips of the drunken fire eaters of The Aura.
The rough guides and maps from your back pack.
The half buried dream of killing your father.
The dog eared copy of Jack's *On The Road*.
The opening chords of some killer rock n roll.
The singular pearl from mother's sea green case.
The sacrifice of the S.I.M. card from your mobile phone.
The tongue moth torn from the mouth of a man of blood.
The dawn of a day that tore the future from its roots.

Then pull out a plum of a carnival compass
that spins the heavy iron in the blood,
points us away from the North's fixed pole,
reversing the polarity to bring this enterprise home.

Where we will sing the salve into hollow hills
realising as always the Sampo has shattered
into formless fragments floating in our wake,
a strung-out trail of flotsam and jetsam,
leaving us with nowt but a needle point
still pricking us to all points North.

Notes

Aino   Joukahainen's younger sister who is pledged to
Vainamoinen, she runs away and drowns, whereupon the
Hare brings the news of her death back to her family.
Nobody knows she is magically transformed into a fish,
Vainamoinen catches her but does not recognise her or she
would change back and marry him. When he goes to cut
her open to investigate the strange fish she flips out
of his hand scolds him, speaks her identity and swims
away forever.

Arto   Invented character not in *Kalevala*. Imagined as
Aino's real sweetheart.

Blue Billy   Nickname given to the ironstone by the
miners of Cleveland ironstone in the Eston Hills due to
the colour of the stone there. At Eston there are remains
of a bronze age hill fort and evidence of earlier activity,
there is also a nineteenth century ghost town on its nearby
moor, now abandoned with nothing remaining except a few
foundations of miners cottages and a well.

Joukahainen   A young wizard bard from Lapland who
challenges Vainamoinen to a bardic battle and loses. In an
attempt to save himself he promises Vainamoinen the hand
of his beautiful sister Aino. Later, following the news of
Aino's death, he attempts to murder Vainamoinen but only
succeeds in setting him adrift in the ocean once more.

Ilmarinen   The primeval smith who forged the heavens
and the first smith to forge iron. Unfortunately the hornet,
working for the evil god Hiisi, added venom to the smelt
to poison it and thereafter iron has always been thirsty for
blood. Vainamoinen, after discovering the origins of iron,

to heal a wound inflicted by an axe, visits Ilmarinen to persuade him to accompany him to Lapland to make the mysterious Sampo for the Northern Witch Queen Louhi in order to win the hand of her daughter the maid of Pohjola.

Kalevala   The epic poem and creation myth which the Finn Elias Lonnrot compiled from folk tales and songs in the 19th Century as part of the Finnish national revival. The name can be interpreted as the 'lands of Kaleva'. The epic consists of 22,795 verses, divided into fifty sections or runo. It contains tales of heroes, wizard—bards, talking animals…adventure, love and tragedy.

Lemminkäinen   Another key hero from later in *Kalevala* who is killed in the whirlpool of the Black River of Tuoni and resurrected by his mother after she reassembles his parts.

Louhi   The Witch Queen of Pohjola, who extracts a promise from Vainamoinen to supply her with The Sampo in exchange for his freedom and her daughter The Maid of Pohjola's hand in marriage.(Ilmarinen wins her instead of Vainamoinen when he is finally tricked and enlisted to help the wizard in his wooing).

Lumiukko   Finnish for Snow Man.

Sampo   A mythical object constructed by Ilmarinen that brought good fortune to its holder; nobody knows exactly what it was supposed to be. When the Sampo was stolen, it is said that Ilmarinen's homeland fell upon hard times and sent an expedition to retrieve it, but in the ensuing battle it was smashed and lost at sea. Similar to the Cornucopia in

Greek Mythology and the Holy Grail in Arthurian Legend.
Sampo is also a word to describe a shaman's drum.

Sisu   A key Finnish term that can be roughly translated
as stamina, strength of will, determination, perseverance,
keeping going no matter what in the face of adversity
and pain.

Tuoni   The god of the underworld, Tuonela, which is
separated from the land of the living by a great black river.

Vainamoinen   The Old Man of Wainola. A primeval
shaman born from his mother after seven years in the
womb, the Ocean, and who floated for thirty more years
before reaching land. A great wizard whose poems sing
the origins of things. Despite his great power he is a
melancholy figure who always loses the girl.

Voipaala   Site of Finnish iron age hill fort in the ancient
kingdom of Rapala. At its foot is an artist's retreat where
the authors have retreated amidst their many poetry tours
of Finland and learned much from Finnish poets and
musicians and floating in the nearby lake.

Acknowledgements

We would like to thank the Finnish poets Ville Hytönen, Kalle Niinikangas, Esa Hirvonen, Tapani Kinnunen, Jenni Haukio, Henri Lehtonen, Riina Katajavuori, Katariina Vuorinen, Marjo Isopahkala, Juha Kulmala, Pauliina Haasjoki, Thurid Erikson of Abo Akademi and Mats Sjostrom for all their advice, support and friendship in the journey to find the Sampo.

Many thanks to Kari and Liisa Niinikangas for all their magnificent hospitality in the Tar House at Voipaala over the years.

Thanks to Jaan Malin, Marja Unt, Eeva Park and everyone in the Estonian Literary Society for helping to take SAMPO to Tallinn and Tartu.

Thanks also to the musicians who have collaborated in the creation of SAMPO as a live performance: Kev Howard, Milo Thelwall, Shaun Lennox, Antti Harma, Masi Hukari, Anton Flint, Dominic Nelson-Ashley, Otso Helasvuo, Aapo Ilves, Santu Karhu and Sara Dennis. Thanks to our lovely wives Louise and Rebecca for putting up with and taking part in our northwards quests.

Thanks also go to the editors of *Perenne's Fountain, The Black Light Engine Room* and *Hullunud Tartu* 2010–2012 in which some of these poems have appeared.

Quotes from the *Kalevala* are from the 1907 translation by W. F. Kirby.

Many thanks to Arts Council England and Teesside University for funding the research, recording and development of these poems.

A CD containing a selection of these poems with music by Gobbleracket is available from www.ekzuban.org.uk